LIE OF THE LAND

Torben Betts

LIE OF THE LAND

in loving memory of
Bill Witcomb
(1945–2008)
who always believed in my voice
when quite a few others did not

OBERON BOOKS
LONDON

WWW.OBERONBOOKS.COM

First published in 2008 by Oberon Books Ltd
521 Caledonian Road, London N7 9RH
Tel: +44 (0) 20 7607 3637 / Fax: +44 (0) 20 7607 3629
e-mail: info@oberonbooks.com
www.oberonbooks.com

A catalogue record for this book is available from the British
Library.

Cover photograph by Adam Barnard

ISBN: 978-1-84002-877-5

Characters

HIM

HER

Setting: a house by the sea

*Inspired by a nightmare that occurred on
Christmas Eve, 2004*

Lie of the Land was first performed at the Pleasance Upstairs, Edinburgh, on 30 July 2008, with the following cast:

HIM, Neal Barry
HER, Nia Gwynne

Director Adam Barnard
Assistant director/Stage manager Eleanor Rhode
Lighting designer Martin Seymour
Sound designer Steve Mayo
Video designer Oscar Sharp

The production then transferred to the Arcola Theatre in London on 6 April 2009 with the actors being replaced by Christopher Harper and Emily Bowker.

SCENE 1

Tartini's The Devil's Trill as Exordium. Bright, fierce sunlight.

Captions with the music:

SCENE THE FIRST: THE BEGINNING OF OUR PLAY.

IN WHICH ONE MAN AND ONE WOMAN, HAVING FLED THE CHAOS OF THE CITY, EMBARK UPON A NEW LIFE IN THE COUNTRY.

IN THIS LITTLE UTOPIA...THE POSSIBILITIES ARE WITHOUT LIMIT.

The music gives way to the sound of waves against a shore.

HIM and HER on, separately spotlit, in sunglasses. They both hold suitcases and stare out in a state of high excitement.

HER: We have inherited a house.

HIM: A house in the country.

HER: A house by the sea.

HIM: And now we are here.

HER: And we are so very…

HIM: …alone.

HER: In love.

HIM: Of course.

HER: With each other.

HIM: So in love and so free and so…

HER: Strong and united after two troubled years.

HIM: When others have cracked.

HER: When they've shattered and split.

HIM: We have survived.

HER: For the rest of our days.

HIM: But I did contribute.

HER: (*After a pause.*) Yes.

HIM: Your family helped out but I did pitch in.

HER: (*After a pause.*) Of course.

The uncaring sea for a time.

HIM: We have come here to be free. To escape the bruising banalities of the modern world.

HER: Its demented, thrashing, blinkered occupants.

HIM: Its crimes and its chaos.

HER: To purge ourselves of fashionable idiocies.

HIM: To disinfect.

HER: With just the wind and the sun and the…uncaring sea.

HIM: So vast. So uncaring. So…indifferent to our…oh, its casual indifference to our…

HER: We need no other in this world. Our quiet devotion to ourselves will almost certainly suffice.

HIM: We have our thoughts and your books and our…quiet devotion.

HER: Beyond the squalid quest for money.

HIM: Beyond the childish thirst for pleasure.

HER: Our new home.

HIM: Our new house in the country.

HER: Our new house by the sea.

The uncaring sea for a time.

HIM: Because I've got a bit of pride, you see? I'm not a one for hand-outs, me... I need to get that straight before... I need to make my own way and... My own way in this wicked world.

The uncaring sea.

Simultaneously they inhale and exhale deeply and contentedly several times.

HER: (*Suddenly excited.*) We shall people this place with children!

HIM: With what?

HER: We shall people this place with little children!

HIM: You're dreaming again.

HER: Little children with golden curls.

HIM: But I'll indulge you one more time.

HER: Oh, I can just imagine them!

HIM: I have no ambition now.

HER: Here and here! And just over here!

HIM: Or was this loss of motivation merely an acceptance of my own failure? No. I shelved my ambitions consciously.

HER: I can almost touch their silky skin and nearly taste their sugared breath.

HIM: I have seen the futility of personal targets and wealth accumulation and have discarded the need to climb the ladder of life.

HER: I no longer dread the future now, I clasp it to my breast!

HIM: Too long have I lived in a terror of death, too long have I lived in a horror of life.

HER: Oh, we are really so blessed to possess all of this.

HIM: I have seen the madness of all worldly endeavour, of seeking status and financial advancement. We shall survive by honest means.

HER: Who'd possibly know if we had just one child?

HIM: Making do will make us noble.

HER: A swing here perhaps?

HIM: I shall reap and I shall sow.

HER: And here perchance a pool?

HIM: I shall finally know what it is to be a man.

HER: A little purple paddling pool.

HIM: I can now rediscover my youthful idealism.

HER: Oh, who needs the city? Who needs the shoving, shouting mob?

HIM: My youthful socialism.

HER: And here, look, boisterous suppers around a long table, the reading of stories, the singing of songs.

HIM: This natural beauty all about me a refuge from despair.

HER: Late-night walks upon the shingle, pebbles hurled into the surf.

HIM: I may be an ordinary man yet I do have the right to a share in all this.

HER: I could cry. Really, I could weep out my soul!

HIM: And I no longer compare. This man's life, that man's career, his salary, his woman, her youth, that chest, the spectacular legs, the way her belly so perfectly…

HER: The air will be full of splashing and giggling. I shall cradle a baby to my bosom.

HIM: I am quite free from all of that.

HER: And watch a toddler lurch through grass.

HIM: And happy with what I have. Happy with the life I've selected.

They turn to each other for a time.

HER: Oh, we're just so very…

HIM: Alone.

HER: And in love.

HIM: With each other.

HER: This is the happiest day of my…

HIM: And God alone knows I have struggled enough.

HER: Our new life begins.

HIM: God alone knows I have struggled for this.

HER: Now. This moment…

HIM: And this moment.

HER: …is all that there is.

HIM: Just listen to the wind through the leaves.

HER: Yes.

They listen.

The wind rustles menacingly through the leaves.

HIM: And the uncaring sea once again.

They listen.

The uncaring sea once again.

A silence.

HER: She only wanted to help.

HIM: I don't want to talk about it.

HER: She only wanted to see us safe.

HIM: I'd rather not discuss.

HER: She was looking out for her daughter.

HIM: You don't understand.

HER: My father would have wanted it.

HIM: But your father was a…

HER: Initially, yes.

HIM: Your father was a…

HER: And then of course he ran for Parliament.

HIM: Your father was an arms dealer!

The uncaring sea for a time.

HER: It is admirable, your sense of honour, of doing as much as you can for yourself. I respect you for it. I love you for it. You who were born with so little in life, you who so understands the meaning of work. It's just that the ways things are now…

HIM: He traded in arms then he stooped for a king.

HER: But still we are doing well, though we may have needed…

HIM: I cannot bear to think of it.

HER: …a little assistance?

HIM: But this is where the healing starts.

HER: Just compare us to the others.

HIM: This is where things all start coming to good.

HER: And it is alright to do that, yes? It is acceptable to be so bold.

HIM: Listen! It has its very own voice! Like it's talking to us! Trying to tell us a secret!

They listen.

The uncaring sea again.

A silence.

HER: Oh, at last, my love, to be away from that city.

HIM: The anonymous city.

HER: Sprawling.

HIM: The city that sprawls.

HER: Its murder.

HIM: Its madness.

HER: Its holes in the road.

HIM: We are sheltered here.

HER: From suicide bombers.

HIM: And poison gas.

HER: So much slaughter under the streets.

HIM: We are in nature, safely.

HER: I shall people this place with children.

HIM: We can now simply be.

HER: Little children.

HIM: No more senior supervisor, no more watching the clock.

HER: I never dreamed that life was…oh…simplicity itself.

HIM: That clock tick-tocking up upon that hated wall, that satanic clock just hanging there and leeching off my days…

HER: One man and one woman, one house by the sea.

HIM: And God alone knows I have struggled enough.

HER: Everything now feels condensed into this…

HIM: God alone knows I have struggled for this.

HER: …this two-person conspiracy against a drowning world.

HIM: At work. Every day. Every moment of every day… someone is watching me. From around a corner, from behind a computer screen. Waiting for me to fail. With an eye on my position. Those above me constantly judging me, silently judging me. Those below me, anxious that I make some error which will…

HER: My darling, my darling, that nightmare has passed.

He calms.

The uncaring sea again.

A silence.

HIM: This sea is beautiful and so are you.

HER: Oh, the hope in your voice now a gift from the gods.

HIM: To live and to die and to miss all of this…

HER: You and I are all the world.

HIM: In the city there was never such a view.

HER: We had the panorama from the top of the block.

HIM: Of the street? The filthy old street.

HER: And all the bars. The bars spilling drunks onto
pavements at night.

HIM: The fist-fights, the Doner kebabs.

HER: The national flags ever fluttering from the windows.

HIM: Litter afloat in the streets in the mornings.

HER: Bodies floating in the mornings also.

HIM: There was litter, there were bodies.

HER: The view here conversely is from quite another world.

HIM: And this grey-green, grey-green, grey-green sea.

HER: Pools of vomit on the stairways also.

HIM: Needles and vomit and puddles of piss.

HER: We lived amongst louts.

HIM: But these were only people who…

HER: The screeching of savages, the dogs, the abuse.

HIM: Troubled, frightened people who…

HER: Look, see that white cloud as it's scudding across!

HIM: I see it scud.

HER: We are in paradise, we are in heaven!

HIM: And yet where are the seabirds?

HER: We can do this, you and I.

HIM: The kittiwakes, cormorants, puffins and terns?

HER: If we trust, if we love.

HIM: I've brought a book on birds, you see.

HIM: Don't you agree?

HIM: I do not know the sea at all. I don't yet know the sea.

HER: And I shall people this place with children.

HIM: In the meantime I shall explore.

HER: Little children.

HIM: Explore the limits of my brand new world.

He explores by pacing up and down.

HER: (*Aside.*) When I look upon this man I see the mirror of
my own need, the embodiment of my own dependency.
A sop he is then, some might say, to my fragile sense of
self-esteem. Though I think I do love him to the core of my
being, I do at night sometimes feel I could have perhaps
aimed a little bit… Oh, but let it go. Let it go. Our wedding
was adequate and my several friends smiled. As a girl I did
dream of a little more glamour but, yes, let it go. One of
my friends even wept. Why do women weep at weddings?
It is from envy surely. The optimism on display there, at
the altar there, it is a rebuke to their own misery, their
inability ever to commit to a life. Yes, this is all I require.
This beauty and this peace. This man. This peace. I have
now clambered clear of my unfortunate beginnings: my
mother's incapacity, my father's lack of love, a daughter
losing out to a political career. And my several friends
smiled. The friends I'll not see but… They did smile. They
think him honest and kind and hard-working though…
poor. Much better than that stockbroker who tore my heart
in two. Yes, they thought I'd waited long enough to have
my moment in the sun… And I know that one of them
does rather covet my situation.

HIM: (*Aside.*) A place to call my own at last, a place to call my very own: acres of land and a house like a palace. Just to look at all this! Just to drink in all this! I'm like a six-year-old on Christmas morning, flying downstairs seven stairs at a time. Like a little boy on Christmas morning. Oh, those Christmas mornings were...they were always so... How they'd struggle and save and then get into debt and... So, Mum, Dad... Look at me now! Not done so bad, now. Just look at all this. Your little man the king of his castle! With a beautifully-spoken princess by his side! And with a view like an emperor, a view like a god. I wish you could... Oh, how I wish you were... But I'm living this for you now, yes? I'm living this dream of existence for you. Look, this, this was the famous Hilltop Farm. The grazing sheep, the dry stone walls. Wisps of white wool snagged up in the barbed wire. Gulls trailing tractors on long summer days. Bluebottles crawling on steaming brown cow shit. I seen the footage. Yes, I seen all the film of this magical place.

HER: (*Aside.*) At the ceremony love hung in the air like so much smog and my snooty old mother as she glanced at the groom, she grimaced at this decent man and...

HIM: (*Returning.*) This is very, very nice, is this!

HER: (*Aside.*) ...she winced at the accent as he stumbled on his vows. Oh, she winced, how she winced, had to wince at the accent.

HIM: It's very, very nice!

HER: But I shall continue to civilise him.

HIM: We will be happy when we settle.

HER: My dress was immaculate and my several friends smiled.

HIM: When we settle in.

HER: But did I in the eyes of some detect a little pity?

HIM: It's nice, is this. It's nice, is this. It's very, very nice, is this.

HER: And what have you discovered?

HIM: A fact.

HER: You have discovered a fact?

HIM: A fact, yes. Or maybe just a…suspicion of one.

HER: Then share it with me, this suspicion. Share it right now with the woman you love.

HIM: This house. This house in the country. This house by the sea. I suspect we shall be happy here.

HER: We shall be happy in our house by the sea?

HIM: When we have settled.

HER: When we have settled, yes.

HIM: When we have settled in our house by the sea. We shall be happy here.

HER: When we have settled in.

HIM: All we need do is settle in.

HER: And then…?

HIM: And then…and then…and then we shall be…happy.

He tries to put down his case. Fails. He looks at her.

She looks at him. She tries to put down her case. Fails.

Then, together, they slowly and cautiously, as if struggling against some unseen force, manage to plant their cases.

They laugh.

The laughter builds.

Lights down.

The Devil's Trill.

SCENE 2

Captions with the music:

SCENE THE SECOND: THE FOLLOWING MORNING.

IN WHICH HE DECIDES TO BURN HIS SUIT…

…AND SHE CONTEMPLATES THE FUTILITY OF ALL HUMAN KNOWLEDGE.

A distant wind is blowing.

Him alone, undressing.

HIM: (*Still in shades.*) I awoke this morning here in this house, in this house in the country, in this house by the sea and, without thinking, I simply dressed into my suit. I dragged a comb right through my matted hair and applied a favourite musk. But this clearly is an act of madness since now I am liberated from all of that. And so…a bonfire. A symbolic burning of these linen fetters. This, a wrinkle-resistant, easy-care broadcloth fabric shirt. Like the skin off my back, you. Like the hair on my head, you. You with the split-back mitred yoke for extra give, you with the single-needle finesse-adding stitched seams, how I have ironed you so mechanically over the years! You machine-washable, low-maintenance blend of polyester and cotton, you shall perish, you shall perish!

He throws the shirt down.

And these trousers made from resilient twill fabric with the soft waistband that neither curls nor pinches and the lined French fly for lasting comfort and the deep side pockets plus the two at the rear and the seven loops to ensure the belt can sit better and the free hemming and what is more…

She enters, also still in shades, reading.

HER: You are incinerating your clothes?

HIM: A burning, yes.

He throws down the trousers.

HER: The alarm went off unkindly.

HIM: Yes.

HER: And I watched you through half-closed eyes as you stooped and you staggered into your suit.

HIM: It was comical.

HER: Yes.

He laughs. Stops suddenly.

She laughs. Stops suddenly.

You need never wear that uniform again.

HIM: No.

HER: We are free.

HIM: In this house in the country.

HER: In this house by the sea.

HIM: And this, this hand-sewn tie made from one hundred per cent Italian silk with the Bemberg lining and the self-fabric keeper loop.

He throws it down.

HER: I am reading a book.

HIM: And oh these shoes, crafted from the finest calf hide for a perfect fit, with a sole which is cured for over a year in oak-lined pits…

HER: It has yet to make an impression.

HIM: …making it highly water resistant, especially breathable and very long-lasting.

He throws the shoes down.

HER: It was written several thousand years ago.

HIM: And this blazer is a timeless classic that would pay dividends on every occasion.

HER: My mother kept it by her bed.

HIM: Lightweight yet substantial, it has a host of multi-functional pockets.

HER: She drummed much of into my innocent mind.

HIM: And you too, you shall singe and you shall blister.

He throws down the blazer.

Behold the husk, the shell of my former life.

HER: A man is made from the soil but grows lonely and so a woman is made for him out of his bones. A serpent then tempts them with everlasting life.

HIM: I am quite moved to look on it now.

HER: They eat some fruit which is strictly out of bounds.

HIM: The years which I lived in its delicate embrace.

HER: Her punishment is agony in childbirth and subordination to man.

HIM: The long dark years in that windowless world.

HER: His is to suffer a lifetime of labour.

HIM: Just consider what we would be doing now. In our former lives.

HER: 'In the sweat of your face you shall eat only bread until the time comes you return to the ground.'

HIM: I picture my colleagues.

HER: Your colleagues?

HIM: I picture them around the water cooler.

HER: Hunched and bent at computers.

HIM: Telling each other what they did at the weekend.

HER: Mouse-clicking, finger-tapping.

HIM: The sport that they watched and the beer that they guzzled.

HER: A coffee break now.

HIM: And the trip underground. In the densely-packed train. Stomach to stomach with sweat-smelling strangers.

The uncaring sea.

Simultaneously they inhale and exhale deeply and contentedly several times.

HER: And so…today? Your plans? Is this the day they are enacted? You're to dig up the garden, to plant out potatoes, to punch through two walls and to unblock the drainage, to look at the boiler, buy some tiles for the roof?

HIM: There is time enough for that.

HER: But, no, no, no! We must live this day as if it were our last! Tomorrow's marked only on the calendars of dreamers, the army of the walking dead with lives unlived and shrivelled souls! We must forget the defeats of yesterday and the problems still to come. This is it! Now! All we have. We must strain every sinew to make it the best day of our lives. This is our time! We must treat everyone we meet, be it friend be it foe, beloved or stranger, as if they die at midnight. Extend to each person, no matter how trivial the contact, all the understanding and the kindness we can muster. We must live now! We must live now! We must live...

She breaks off, spent.

They do not speak.

The uncaring sea.

The wind.

She calms.

HIM: There is time enough for digging the garden.

HER: Yes.

HIM: We must first settle in.

HER: We must first settle in.

HIM: In this our large house.

HER: Our house in the country.

HIM: Our house by the sea.

They do not speak.

The uncaring sea.

The wind.

But for now let us just be together. Alone together. Just you and I and the uncaring sea and the rolling hills and the air so pure and the sun so strong and us all alone and all will be well and all will be good in this our large house, our large house in the country, our large house by the sea...

They do not speak.

The uncaring sea.

The wind.

She closes her eyes.

What are you thinking?

HER: My thoughts aren't my own?

HIM: Of course they are.

They do not speak.

The uncaring sea.

The wind.

HER: I am plotting a novel.

HIM: You've always talked about it.

HER: Now I have the time and the space a novel is what I'll write.

HIM: We can live simply, creatively.

HER: It will expose my late father for the fraud that he was. My mother for the fool.

HIM: But the house…? Won't she…?

HER: The deeds are in our name.

HIM: But you should never bite the hand that feeds.

They do not speak.

The uncaring sea.

The wind.

He closes his eyes.

HER: And what are you thinking?

HIM: My thoughts aren't my own?

HER: Of course they are.

They do not speak.

The uncaring sea.

The wind.

HIM: I am plotting the garden.

HER: That's good.

HIM: We shall be self-sufficient.

HER: And we shall not kill.

HIM: No. We shall not kill.

HER: Then we shall live forever.

HIM: Yes.

HER: We need no other.

HIM: You and I are all the world.

They do not speak.

The uncaring sea.

The wind.

The silence in the end becomes too much.

HER: (*Suddenly excited.*) A walk to the village perhaps? And
then to a pub?

HIM: (*Suddenly excited.*) Yes! Yes! We must introduce ourselves.

HER: To the neighbours.

HIM: Become a part of the landscape.

HER: But wait. I grew up in a small town. Do I like that scene? That scene so small. So suffocating. So suffocating small. With people who know each other, from cradle to tomb, intimate, eyes all-seeing…and peering over fences and curtains twitching and…

HIM: Become…acquainted.

HER: And when we enter their faces will turn to the door, we'll be looked up and down and a silence will fall…

HIM: Too long have we lived all alone in a crowd.

HER: But wait. I grew up in a small town. Do I like that scene? That scene so small. So suffocating. So suffocating small.

HIM: We have escaped the cold anonymity of the city, the loneliness of the urban life and now at last…visibility. Responsibility. The chance to belong.

HER: I am nervous of it.

HIM: We should shake their toil-toughened fists. Real work, this, in the salty, open air, not simple office drudgery, not life inside a cage.

HER: But I am from the capital!

HIM: We should work at being welcome here.

HER: I know about literature and philosophy. I have a more than passing interest in contemporary art.

HIM: We should support the community.

HER: But what will I say? The words will snag in my throat. My tongue will be as a trowel through ashes in my mouth. Oh, that dreadful collapse of articulation will descend upon me. I am always so reticent in the face of backslapping banter. I will not understand the dialect, I'm sure. Oh, all that cackling in crowds. I simply never get the joke.

A very long silence.

No. Please. There is time enough for that.

HIM: When we've settled in.

They look at the heap of clothing on the ground for a time.

HER: Torch it.

HIM: No looking back.

HER: We shall live without regret.

HIM: No looking down.

He crouches down. Takes a lighter from his pocket.

The heap burns.

The sound of fire and an orange glow.

He watches the fire.

She reads her book. Turns a page.

VOICE: The Lord saw how great man's wickedness on the earth had become, and that every inclination of the thoughts of his heart was only to evil all of the time. The Lord was grieved that he had made man on the earth, and his heart was filled with pain. So the Lord said, 'I will wipe mankind, whom I have created, from the face of the earth – men and animals, and creatures that move along the ground, and all the birds of the air – for I am grieved that I have made them.'

HER: (*Snapping the book shut.*) Reading is not living. No. It is merely a second-rate substitution for it. (*Tossing the book onto the fire.*) And we came here, did we not, to embrace life? To live it to the full.

She holds out her hand to him.

He takes it.

They watch the fire.

HIM: Wait!

He shoots his hand into the fire, reacts to the pain, and retrieves the book.

They look at each other.

Lights down.

The Devil's Trill.

SCENE 3

Captions with the music:

SCENE THE THIRD: SOME TIME HAVING PASSED.

IN WHICH HE DISCOVERS A PASSION FOR LOCAL HISTORY...

...AND SHE RELIVES THE WONDERFUL FREEDOMS OF HER CHILDHOOD.

A beach. The uncaring sea much closer. The wind stronger. She is alone, engaged in T'ai-Chi. She inhales deeply.

HER: I breathe in all that is iniquitous in this world.

She breathes out deeply and slowly.

And now, having transformed this malevolent energy into a breath that is pure, I release it back into the air.

She breathes in deeply and then breathes out likewise.

What are all the others doing? I feel for all the others in their brutal working world.

She closes her eyes and the stage is filled with the sounds of the working world.

Lights down on her and up on him.

The sounds of the working world are replaced by the buzzing of flies and the babble of a river.

He is reading and fishing.

HIM: Rainbow trout. I'm sitting here and waiting for the rainbow trout to bite. I smile to myself, as I sit here on this soft, green bank, the leaves of this massive oak shielding me from the blazing eye of heaven above. I laugh. (*He laughs.*) This is such an act of rebellion. I am perhaps being rewarded for my courage. I have said…enough, no more. I shall not waste my precious moments like that. And God alone knows I have suffered enough. God alone knows I have suffered for this. I shall read. I shall educate myself and I shall fish for rainbow trout. I feel for the first time in my adult life…what is the word?…contented. I am at ease. I am idle and free. And what are all the others doing? I feel for all the others in their brutal working world.

He closes his eyes and the stage is once again filled with the sounds of the working world.

Lights down on him and up on her.

The sounds cease.

HER: God did not make us to live in this way. The madness of the urban crowd. How we fretted in the gridlock. How we seethed and we cursed in the car and the train. House prices, problems with storms and with flooding. Snouts in the dailies, in office and classroom, whilst outside these cages the angry sun blazes, blazes and scorches off all of that concrete, all of that glass. But here, here, no need for newspapers here, no need for the television. How anyway alter the course of this world? I have put away my novel now since what is artistic creation but the psychotic twitchings of disordered minds? What need have I to write a single word? I am at ease. I am idle and free. We must learn to stand still merely and appreciate the wonders around us. Slow our bodies right down to a heartbeat, a pulse.

She closes his eyes and the stage is once again filled with the sounds of the working world.

Lights down on her and up on him.

The sounds cease.

HIM: The world is full of death and shouting.

His line is tugged.

Ah! Now! This will be my very first fish. I need no handbook but will angle from instinct. This is how the ancients existed! I will lure the creature toward me with the power of my spirit and then live like a native. I, the hunter, I the protector of those whom he loves. I will feed her, the gatherer, I will nourish her, I will be a man of the land.

The line is tugged again.

I respect you, o trout. I respect you but I will kill you. Your life and mine are intertwined. I will catch you, I will eat you and I will shit you out upon the earth and there you will live again, there you will feed this soil, this grass, these shimmering daffodils, and your energy, the energy against which I am currently battling, it will once again become a part of this rich and beautiful landscape.

He tugs at his line and then pulls out a human skull.

Lights down on him and up on her.

HER: I feel like a little one again. I feel somewhat euphoric, as if all my cares were being washed away by these waves. Ah, a sea shell. I remember collecting them as a child. Oh, the innocence, the joy of it all. When days seemed to last forever and yes, each moment an eternity crammed full of adventure and surprise.

She picks up the shell.

I do believe my faith is returning. My mother's
Christianity. The certainties I clung to as an anxious little
girl.

She holds it up.

A flash of light.

Music.

A vision of God. It fades.

*Lights down on her and up on him, holding up the skull in one hand,
the book in the other.*

The sounds of marching, singing.

HIM: A thousand years ago the soldiers came. They were
marching for God, marching for the King, marching for
the fields of England. And they climbed up there singing.
Where that copse stands sentinel upon the hill, they
pitched their tents. Looking down at this river. Singing.
Cold, hungry and scared for their lives, but still they sang.
Why do soldiers sing so as they trudge to their extinction?
Drawn from the outlying towns and villages, paying their
rent for the huts that they lived in, they sat around fires
at the crest just there, looking down at this brook as it
peacefully babbled by. And there they awaited the dawn.

Lights down on him and up on her.

The marching and singing still.

HER: It is all so much greater than I. I dissolve into God's
greatness and am swept away. My ego as nothing,
aspirations evaporating, like dew in the morning sun. It is
like a death. And in this death is freedom. My fears and
regrets, they are merely illusion, all hopes and all dreams
they are simply delusion. It is now just the uncaring sea.
And the burning sun. And the roaring wind.

A silence.

The sound of men screaming in battle, the clashing of swords.

Lights down on her and up on him.

HIM: And when it broke they appeared over the brow, fifteen thousand men, banners trembling in the morning breeze, crows cawing, dark and menacing shapes flying against the cold autumn skyline. Barefoot they came to gain some grip on these muddy slopes. A mass of pikes, moving in one imposing line, down, down towards this river. And then the artillery started on them. Cannonballs pulverising flesh and bone, punching holes through all the human tissue. And then the longbows unleashed their arrows. By noon it had started to rain. And as it came down with these showers of arrows, men writhed and choked in the mud, impaled through throat and chest and gut. The armies clashed just here, the fighting, brutal, furious, intense, men screaming with fear and rage and pain, with the blades of the billmen tearing at tendons and hacking at faces. Men fell in their thousands and were slaughtered where they fell. By dusk these fields a sea of naked, bleeding bodies, the screams of dying men echoing through the valley and this river, this picture of serenity here, was gorged with blood, with floating limbs and severed heads and corpses packed so tightly that they served as a bridge from one bank to the other.

Lights down on him and up on her.

HER: I am like a newborn, my being quivering with gratitude. Beyond the clutches of the system, beyond the clutches of my ego, I swim in blissful selflessness, in being attached to nothing at all and to no-one at all.

Lights down on her and up on him.

HIM: All night they dug. As the last of the day disappeared over the horizon, they dug by torchlight. And they lugged the dead over the bleeding earth and the wet grass and piled them high. Stripped of clothes and possessions they were tossed into a pit. Ten thousand men. A mound of naked, massacred men and teenage boys. Stomachs exposed, ribs jutting from chests, blood-red bodies, blood-red and butchered. There to rot, forgotten, forgotten. There to rot, forgotten.

Lights down on him and up on her.

She is moving slowly around the stage.

The Devil's Trill fades in again.

HER: And I dance as I danced in my miserable youth, I'm thinking of nothing, I am only the dance. And the childminder's there, that fat girl from the Balkans, she's watching the dance from the back of the room, my father's away shaking hands with his sheiks, it's Tartini that's playing, I'm dressed all in pink with my pigtails, my pigtails so perfectly done. Just look, I am flying, be proud of me, proud. The others, the others…like hippos compared. I'm like the air while they stagger and drop, they stagger and stumble like miniature drunkards in huge hobnailed boots.

He enters, holding a bag. Nonplussed he watches her for a time.

The music fades.

HIM: Rainbow trout. I suggest grilled with bay leaves and lemon. Or what about baked with tomatoes and a piquant caper sauce?

She breaks off, exhausted. Stares at him in disbelief.

HER: What have you done?

HIM: Due to the inherent tastelessness of all freshwater fish I affirm that you need something tart, something with a little flavour, to make the whole dining experience even remotely worthwhile.

HER: You have caught it yourself?

HIM: I landed it like an amateur, though one with beginner's luck. I hoisted it onto the bank and then, as it writhed and it flapped, with a very large stone I pounded its brains till all slithering stopped.

HER: You have murdered this fish?

HIM: (*After a pause.*) Yes.

HER: You have contravened the law of life.

HIM: But man has always...

HER: We agreed we are the world. The future is us. We have wiped the past clean and you and I, we were to dispense with all killing.

HIM: You repudiate my trout?

HER: We are the rebirth of mankind and there shall be no death here for there was no death in Paradise. Man lived in peace with the birds and the...

HIM: This trout would have died in the end and so...

HER: There's been slaughter enough in this terrible world!

HIM: (*Aside.*) Have I betrayed my class then, tell me? Have I compromised my politics?

HER: (*Aside.*) Oh, give me back my freedom. Restore to me my solitude. But when he is gone, when he is gone, always this ache of isolation. I need him but resent him for the fact of it. Could he not possibly do any better than me? Oh, what to do? Tell me what it is that I want in this world?

She resumes her T'ai-Chi.

Think deeply about what you have done.

HIM: A resentment brews.

HER: Then let it pass.

HIM: The river is devoid of fish. Not one living thing did I see the whole day.

HER: The river is devoid?

HIM: I don't have a trout.

HER: You don't have a trout?

HIM: And God alone knows we are hungry enough.

HER: So you didn't then kill?

HIM: There's no blood on these hands.

HER: I am so very pleased.

He begins copying her.

Do you feel at peace?

HIM: Not really.

HER: Then what do you feel?

HIM: Hunger and regret.

HER: Hunger and regret?

HIM: I think of my boyhood. The joy of my boyhood. The lack of concern. The loving people all around.

HER: You must feel no regret. You must feel no fear.

HIM: But I fear death. Oh, how I fear death. Although we know no more than do the cattle as to what lies beyond the grave. I fear the passing of the days. To be like the beasts, unburdened by time, it is a thought most delightful to the mind. And yet I cling, cling most abjectly to this life. I miss the city.

HER: Do not say it.

HIM: Take me back to the life of the city.

HER: All life is here, my love.

HIM: I need the struggle, the anger of the fight.

HER: Oh, but think of the competition…

HIM: I see young couples kissing…

HER: Here is Nirvana, think of those fumes…

HIM: A steak cooked with mustard.

HER: The carbon monoxide…

HIM: A full, red Rioja.

HER: The dingy apartments.

HIM: A night at the pictures.

HER: When we have all this.

HIM: A day at the races.

He topples over.

They do not speak.

The uncaring sea.

The wind.

All I am then is this emptiness? All I am then is this loneliness? This is not me? I am a person, yes? A thinking reaction to all of this chaos! But I look into myself and what do I find? What is there inside that I can say: yes, this is ME? This is who I am? Nothing. Only the memory of floating sensations, just little scraps of rumour in a waste of forgotten time. It is like the grave…this peace, this peace is death. This peace, this silence it is nothing but a slow, slow death!

She hands him the shell.

(*Tearful.*) I pass my life as in a dream. A dream from which I can't awake.

HER: Just listen to what it tells you. Just listen to the voice of God.

He takes the shell. He holds it to his ear.

He listens.

The terrifyingly loud sound of jet aircraft.

He turns to her.

She smiles.

He hands back the shell.

Lights down.

The Devil's Trill.

SCENE 4

Captions with the music:

SCENE THE FOURTH: A CHRISTMAS EVE SOME TIME LATER.

IN WHICH SHE ATTEMPTS TO SIT STILL AND HE ATTEMPTS TO REDISCOVER HIS SOCIALISM...

...EVEN AS THE FINAL CRISIS IS COMING UPON THEM.

A storm raging outside.

The lighting flashing on and off. It is Christmas Eve.

A tree.

She sits alone in silence. After a time she becomes restless.

HER: The root cause of mankind's misery is he can't sit quietly in a room on his own.

She attempts to sit still. After a time she becomes restless.

Teach us to care and not to care. Teach us to sit still.

She attempts to sit still. After a time she becomes restless.

Silence is deep as Eternity, speech is as shallow as Time.

She attempts to sit in silence. After a while she becomes restless. She remotes the TV, its flickering light illuminating her face.

TV: '…that it's safe to say, I'm afraid, that the wars have now finally begun. The scene here is one of utter chaos. When in years past Oxford Street was dominated by Christmas lighting, now lifeless bodies are floating everywhere and the water is crimson with blood. Gang warfare is rife in this city now and the flood barriers are powerless to stem the ever-rising water levels. The handful of kind souls prepared to venture outside and try to help are simply being picked off by the…'

She switches off the TV.

Light change. A deep silence falls.

HER: Do not, Loneliness, do not think…do not think for a second that you are winning. (*A slight laugh.*) Oh no. Not winning, no. I can and I shall overcome your… relentless… your…relentless…

A deep silence. She struggles with it. She switches the TV back on.

Light change.

TV: '…seems to be every man for himself. Sections of what's left of the media are already calling this the Endgame. It's certainly the final Land Grab we've long been expecting and those fortunate enough, or wealthy enough, to already live on higher ground are being warned that they will probably now have to defend their homes and to defend them with their lives.'

She switches off the TV. Light change. A deep silence falls.

HER: What are you? What are you but a voice from the city? What do you have to do with me? Give me rather this… this peace, this silence…it soothes me. Yes, it soothes me… quite.

A deep silence. She struggles with it.

She switches the TV back on.

Light change.

TV: '…which will largely be felt in coastal areas. The effect of these storms may well be extremely severe, indeed the winds are reaching unprecedented hurricane force in some parts of, what we can now accurately call, the archipelago. The Meteorological Office is advising all commercial shipping to postpone any…'

Suddenly the TV explodes.

Light change. A deep silence falls.

She sighs.

HER: The television is dead. The television has died. This is good. Yes. This is a sign perhaps? The television has finally died. The television has now disappeared forever.

She sits in silence in the darkness, lights flickering on and off, the storm raging outside. After a time:

Oh…this is simply too much. I shall…I shall… Presently I shall fill this solitude, this emptiness, this merciless absence of, this pitiless absence of… Yes, I shall fill it with the hungry screaming of just one more generation…

A door is opened, the sound of the storm increases. It closes, it decreases.

He now enters. He is soaked, in a raincoat, carrying a torch.

She leaps to her feet.

He takes off the coat to reveal a political rosette on his lapel.

Where have you been? I have been so alone, so unremittingly…

HIM: I have signed up to a group.

HER: A group?

HIM: A political group.

HER: A political group?

HIM: A political group. Yes. I am however the only member.

HER: But what about me?

HIM: I have joined one alone.

HER: Alone without me?

HIM: Alone without you.

HER: Of which persuasion this political group?

HIM: (*After a pause.*) That I can't say.

HER: But I should like to join a group.

HIM: You have no politics.

HER: And neither have you.

The silence.

Proceed then? Your politics please?

HIM: There is…injustice.

HER: Yes?

HIM: And inequality.

HER: But wait…

HIM: The rich prey upon the poor.

HER: But we are the rich.

HIM: The poor are all around us.

HER: And we mean them no harm.

HIM: It is time to act.

HER: You have joined a group?

HIM: Indeed I have.

HER: But you, you, you are the rich.

HIM: I have become restless.

HER: Restless?

HIM: People are dying.

HER: You have no politics.

HIM: And neither have you.

> *The sound of jet aircraft overhead.*

> *They cower.*

HIM: I wish they would fly at a higher altitude.

HER: How can they when their job is to target the enemy?
Carpet bombing is inappropriate in all cases.

HIM: But the noise.

HER: They are out on manoeuvres. It's a comforting sound.

HIM: They ruin the peace of the country, the shore.

HER: They are practising. They are spirited men.

HIM: Yes.

HER: Attractive young men in that excellent kit. I sleep better at night with the thought they are there.

They do not speak.

The storm rages.

A political meeting?

HIM: We must certainly act.

HER: But you have no politics.

HIM: And neither have you.

They do not speak.

Only the storm.

There is nothing to be done. There is nothing to be said.

HER: We could always play a parlour game?

HIM: But I shall be your barricade.

HER: I had a talent for charades.

HIM: I shall look after you.

HER: Such a talent for that game…

A long silence falls.

The storm outside.

They regard each other.

Eventually he takes a book from his coat and starts to read.

Please. Put it down.

HIM: But I still need to read.

HER: No.

HIM: I have got as far as history, philosophy.

HER: I need your company.

HIM: But I need to learn quickly. While there's still time.

HER: No more reading, no, no, no!

He lowers the book.

A long silence falls.

The storm outside.

They regard each other.

You are silent.

HIM: As are you.

HER: But your silence is…

HIM: The same as your silence.

HER: No. Your silence is quite different.

HIM: Our silences are similar.

HER: Your silence is threatening.

HIM: I threaten no-one with my silence.

HER: Your silence threatens me.

HIM: If my silence threatens you then it is nothing to do with me.

HER: Of course your silence is to do with you.

HIM: The silence exists. I do not create it.

HER: Your silence is…menacing. Male.

HIM: My silence is menacing?

HER: Yes.

> *They do not speak.*

> *The storm outside.*

> *They regard each other.*

There. Again. You are hostile.

HIM: Hostile?

HER: You are hostile with your lack of speech. Your refusal to…articulate.

HIM: You lacked speech also.

HER: I was waiting for you.

HIM: And I was waiting for you.

HER: And yet you were silent.

HIM: As silent as you.

HER: Your silence is cruel.

HIM: I had nothing to say.

> *They do not speak.*

> *Only the storm.*

HER: Will you please kiss me? I need the solace of a kiss.

HIM: You need the solace of a kiss?

HER: I need the solace of a kiss.

> *They regard each other for a time.*

> *Only the storm.*

The television is no more.

HIM: The television is no more?

HER: The television has died a death.

Only the storm.

HIM: The village is flooded, deserted, forsaken.

HER: But I need the solace of a kiss.

HIM: But we can make things better still. We can improve these people's lives.

The silence builds as they regard each other.

Only the storm.

HER: I need the solace of a kiss.

HIM: The television is dead?

HER: I need the solace of a kiss.

HIM: You said the television is dead?

HER: If you would be so kind.

HIM: (*Aside as they kiss.*) Like pebbles clashing.

HER: (*Aside as they kiss.*) His lips like wet bark.

HIM: Her tongue barely ventures from the cave of her jaw.

HER: His breath always fusty.

HIM: When once it slithered and flicked.

HER: Like cold chops and cabbage.

HIM: When once it probed and it prodded.

HER: Like socks long unwashed.

The silence builds as they regard each other.

Only the storm.

I have come to a conclusion tonight…while you have been out, out at your meeting, your political event…

HIM: You have been coming to conclusions?

A silence.

HER: I now require…

HIM: Yes?

HER: To make me happy I require…

HIM: Yes?

HER: I now categorically require…an infant.

A long silence.

He begins to pace.

What are you doing?

HIM: I am pacing with anxiety.

He continues to pace.

(*Aside.*) I was alone when we met. Alone in the world. Adrift. Those evenings alone. And alone I would drink. My friends grew a bore to me and I one to them. We reminded each other of our own desolation. We were trapped together in a mutual need. Gang-making. And then she…oh, and then she…

HER: Everything will then just fall into place.

HIM: She drifted like a dream into my days.

HER: I shall parent now. I shall certainly…parent.

HIM: And all became clear.

HER: I was alone when we met.

HIM: I abandoned my friends for…

HER: Adrift. Alone. Those evenings alone.

HIM: …the taste of her body, that undiscovered meat.

HER: My friends grew a bore to me and I one to them.

HIM: The violence of her kissing.

HER: We reminded each other of our own desolation.

HIM: Her lips crushing, her hips bucking.

HER: We were trapped together in a mutual need. Gang-making.

HIM: Her extraordinary haunches.

HER: I fled from them to him.

HIM: Her talons clawing at my flesh. Her moaning like grief.

HER: The sweet anaesthetic of his company.

HIM: Like one whose sons lie under rubble.

HER: The narcotic of his attention.

HIM: But now…but now…

HER: Yes, he wrenched me free.

He stops pacing.

Your conclusion then?

HIM: We are happy here. The two of us. Now that we have settled.

HER: But it is time to expand our love.

HIM: In our house in the country, in our house by the sea.

HER: To share this happiness with another creature.

HIM: But it's against all the regulations!

The sound of a jet aircraft overhead.

He resumes his pacing.

(*Aside.*) And I have as yet done so little of value in this world. I have taken merely. I have consumed merely. I need to make a lasting mark.

HER: (*Aside.*) An infant will fill up all these empty hours.

HIM: (*Aside.*) But instead some cul-de-sac of caring.

HER: (*Aside.*) Eyes of unconditional love will sparkle up at me.

HIM: (*Aside.*) One long corridor of concerns.

HER: (*Aside.*) The problems of the world will for me be quite…obliterated.

HIM: (*Aside.*) My potential slowly drip-drip-dripping away.

He stops.

They face each other.

HER: Then it is decided.

HIM: And then the dilemma of the children's education.

HER: An infant is what we need.

HIM: The guilty dilemma of the children's education.

Loud knocking suddenly.

In terror they stare at each other.

The knocking again.

HER: This is something we imagine, yes?

HIM: Something we invent?

The knocking again.

Perhaps it is a neighbour?

HER: A neighbour?

HIM: Or a victim of the system?

The knocking again.

They again regard each other cautiously.

HER: We must answer the knocks.

HIM: Yes.

HER: It may well be someone less fortunate than ourselves.

HIM: A victim of the system.

HER: After all it's Christmas Eve.

The knocking again.

They approach the door.

HIM: There was someone.

HER: Yes?

HIM: An old musician. By the church.

HER: An old musician by the church?

HIM: He stood in the rain, by the porch of the church, the
water right up to his scrawny old chest. I rowed quickly
by and he turned to me slowly. I smiled quite politely and
then looked away. His expression was one of elation and…

HER: Describe him to me.

HIM: Impossibly old and impossibly tall.

HER: We must save him from the storm.

HIM: I suggested he join us. He join us for tonight.

HER: You invited a guest?

HIM: He is a victim of the system.

HER: But we have not entertained for many, many years.

HIM: And he was playing the violin. A look so bizarre on his wizened old face, even as the river rose up to his neck, his smile was a smile of both triumph and sadness… And then as his head sunk beneath the cold water, he kept drawing the bow with skill over his head.

Cautiously the door is opened and the storm rages wildly.

They go out into it, nervously. She has to struggle against the storm, her voice fighting against the wind.

HER: You are welcome here! Don't suffer in this night! Reveal yourself to us! What we have here is basic only: a little light, a little heat, a little…television. Nothing beyond! We long since abandoned our unpretentious car!

Only the storm.

We have been waiting for you patiently and it's time for you to come! We have learned from all our errors now!

Only the storm.

We have tried so hard to be good! We are innocent, believe us! So have we perhaps then been chosen? Because we do love each other! The two of us. We love each other very much! What more can we do? What more can we do this in this life that you gave us?! Come out of the rain now!

Only the storm.

It is safe in inside and it is secure! Surely you cannot begrudge us both that?!

Only the storm.

Let us forget about the past! What is done is done! Shouldn't we all simply look to the future?! Come celebrate our Christmas here, come celebrate our life with us!

Only the storm. It increases in its rage.

Lights down.

The Devil's Trill.

SCENE 5

Captions with the music:

SCENE THE FIFTH: THAT SAME STORMY EVENING.

IN WHICH THEY WAIT FOR THEIR FIRST GUEST TO ARRIVE...

...AND OUR LITTLE PLAY THEN DRAWS TO ITS CLOSE.

The storm wild.

She is laying an imaginary table.

He is reading.

Both have on red Santa hats.

They have to raise their voices to be heard above the storm.

HER: The table must always be immaculately laid.

HIM: Human history has no meaning, it seems.

HER: The napkins freshly laundered.

HIM: It makes no sense at all.

HER: The table linen clean, the candles pristine, new.

HIM: Cycles of growth and of wars and decline.

HER: The silverware polished.

HIM: Humanity a myth, progress just a myth.

HER: The glasses all gleaming.

HIM: There is nothing but foolishness within the heart of man.

HER: The placement of guests is so hugely important.

HIM: But there is only the one.

HER: The host should sit at the head of the table…

HIM: There is just the one.

HER: …and the hostess at the foot…

HIM: And he is not coming.

HER: Couples are separated.

HIM: There are none.

HER: Guests should be arranged in a boy/girl sequence.

HIM: The only couple is us.

HER: Place cards should always be hand-written.

HIM: One guest is all.

HER: In fountain pen.

HIM: Only one guest. Just one guest is all.

The shattering of glass.

HER: The centrepiece could be a bowl of perfect fruit…

HIM: We have no fruit.

HER: …an ornament perhaps or just a vase of flowers.

HIM: Neither have we flowers.

HER: Flowers however should not be too fragrant…

HIM: Since the bees have all abandoned us.

HER: …as they can interfere with the aroma of the food.

HIM: We have no food to serve.

HER: The most simple folding of a napkin is twice…

HIM: It is time for us to see things as they actually are.

HER: …to form a perfect square.

HIM: We are alone.

HER: Lay glasses last to avoid knocking them over.

HIM: Our guest does not appear to be coming…

HER: They are placed on the right-hand side of the setting…

HIM: …to share our Christmas feast.

HER: …just above the dinner knife…

HIM: Perhaps it's time to accept…

HER: …and are arranged from front to back in the order in which they will be used…

HIM: …that we're in this alone.

HER: …or in little clusters even.

HIM: Let us no longer dream of overcoming ourselves.

HER: The water glass is placed slightly behind and on the left of the wine glasses.

The shattering of glass.

HIM: Perhaps I didn't even see the man?

HER: I have always loved Christmas.

HIM: Perhaps it was illusion?

HER: Always longed to play the host.

HIM: The night was dark, my mind was fevered.

HER: He is our Saviour and he is without doubt to be with us tonight!

HIM: He will not save us!

HER: I know that he will!

HIM: Deliver us please from this long line of Saviours!

HER: You are reading, not living!

HIM: It seems he's not coming.

HER: Because you, you, you do not believe! You do not believe!

They do not speak for a time.

The storm, the lightning.

There. All done. So how do I look?

HIM: You are beautiful.

HER: I am beautiful?

HIM: You are beautiful and I love you.

HER: Our guest, it would appear, is now certainly late.

The shattering of glass.

It is a long time since we had company.

HIM: A very long time.

HER: You've been all that I needed…

HIM: And you've been all that I...

> *The shattering of glass.*

> *They do not speak.*

> *The storm building outside.*

HER: It is a long time since we had company.

HIM: A very long time.

> *They do not speak.*

> *The storm building outside.*

HER: Our guest, it would appear, is now certainly late.

HIM: Yes.

HER: We have been waiting for many, many hours.

HIM: And the table is immaculate.

HER: Our guest, it would appear, is now certainly late.

> *The shattering of glass.*

> *The storm rages.*

> Perhaps he has forgotten.

HIM: Double-booked? Yes.

HER: The engagement may even have slipped his ageing mind.

HIM: It would be the height of bad manners.

HER: Either way: a colossal impertinence.

HIM: When we have acted...

HER: ...from the kindness of our...

HIM: When we have opened up our...

HER: …hearts!

HIM: And our home!

HER: When we have opened up our home!

HIM: To a man all alone!

HER: In this season of…

HIM: …cheer!

HER: Of good will to all men!

The shattering of glass.

The storm rages.

They do not speak for some time.

Why won't you speak then?

HIM: I have nothing to say!

HER: You have nothing to say?

HIM: I have nothing to say!

The storm rages.

They do not speak for some time.

HER: Why won't you speak then?

HIM: I have nothing to say!

The shattering of glass.

The storm rages.

They do not speak for some time.

HER: Do you not have an opinion?

He throws down his book.

HIM: What are my words but the splutterings of an unfocused mind! Half-truths distilled from a wilderness of pages!

HER: We have many convictions!

HIM: All this solitary reading!

HER: We know about life!

HIM: There is nothing that we do not know at this time!

The shattering of glass.

The storm rages.

They do not speak for some time.

HER: Tell me something new then!

HIM: I have nothing to say!

HER: Tell me something… bizarre! Be fresh!

HIM: There is nothing I could say that you have not been told before!

HER: Our guest, it would appear, is now certainly late!

The storm rages.

It is essential that we stick together!

HIM: Essential!

HER: You and I!

HIM: Alone!

HER: Together!

HIM: In this our house!

HER: Our house in the country!

HIM: Our house by the sea!

The storm rages.

They do not speak for some time.

Our guest, it would appear, is now certainly late!

The storm.

HIM: Perhaps he was caught in the storm!

HER: These hurricane winds!

HIM: Perhaps he did drown?

HER: He may have been knocked off his feet!

HIM: Another victim of the system…

HER: Crushed by a tree or impaled on a branch!

HIM: I would have listened to his concerns!

HER: The story of our lives!

HIM: The concerns of the dispossessed man!

HER: We would on occasions have sniggered together!

HIM: The ordinary, ordinary man!

HER: We are all the same species.

HIM: Would have listened and been concerned!

HER: We are all the same beast!

The storm rages.

The shattering of glass.

Our guest, it would appear, is now certainly late!

Suddenly the storm ceases.

An eerie silence descends.

They stand in terror and excitement.

The distant strains of The Devil's Trill.

Gradually the violin music draws closer as if the violinist were slowly approaching the house.

They hold hands in terror.

The music draws closer still.

Slow footsteps.

This is it. He is coming for us now.

HIM: Hear me, oh mothers, hear me, oh fathers! Our fathers and mothers who lived in such comfort. I shall not now worship you, nor pray for your help! No, I'll condemn you with all of my heart!

He wildly thrashes at the air in anger.

Six…for indifference! Six…for stupidity! Six…for self-centredness beyond the reach of words…

The music draws closer still.

Slow footsteps.

And for what?! And for what? And so tell me please for what? To sacrifice your children, oh for just a little…

HER: He is coming.

HIM: For just a little…

HER: He is coming now.

HIM: Ease.

The violin music stops abruptly.

The door swings open.

The storm has passed and the stage is flooded with bright fierce sunlight again.

The sound of the waves more calmly against the shore.

They step outside, simultaneously putting their sunglasses back on. They scour the scene in awe and wonder.

HER: Boats.

HIM: Rafts.

HER: A thousand of them.

HIM: As far as the eye can see.

HER: Our fellow man.

HIM: They're coming closer. They're drawing near.

HER: To rescue us.

HIM: To save our troubled souls.

Still in their red Santa hats, they both begin smiling and waving hopefully, desperately.

BOTH: Here! Here! Over here! Over here!

As they wave, the lights gradually fade to black and the sounds of violence and war slowly overwhelm them.